Mother Teresa of Calcutta and Her Life of Charity

Kids Biography Books Ages 9-12
Children's Biography Books

BABY PROFESSOR
EDUCATION KIDS

Speedy Publishing LLC
40 E. Main St. #1156
Newark, DE 19711
www.speedypublishing.com
Copyright 2017

*M*other Teresa was known as a humanitarian who devoted her life to assisting the sick, the helpless, the poor, and the needy. While she was known as a humanitarian, there was criticism of her accomplishments as you will read later in this book.

Saint Teresa of Calcutta was a Catholic Nun born in Uskub, Ottomon on August, 26, 1910 and died in Calcutta, India on September 5, 1997. She was beatified by the Catholic Church, which is one step towards becoming a Saint. She is now referred to as Blessed Teresa of Calcutta.

Skopje

Where did she grow up?

....

She was born in Uskub, Ottoman Empire which is now known as Skopje, which is the Republic of Macedonia's capital city. She was named Agnes Gonxa Bojaxhiu at birth.

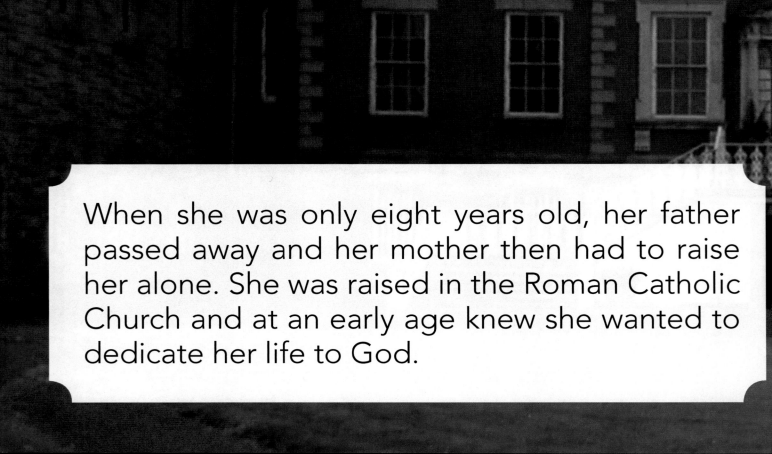

When she was only eight years old, her father passed away and her mother then had to raise her alone. She was raised in the Roman Catholic Church and at an early age knew she wanted to dedicate her life to God.

She joined with the Sisters of Loreto at the age of 18, becoming a missionary to India. Prior to being able to go to England, she was required to learn the English language. She attended Loreto Abby in Ireland for a year in order to learn the language.

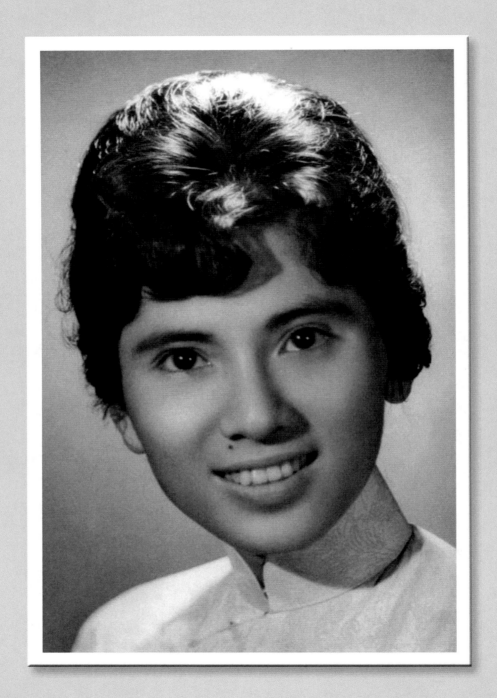

Agnes then began her work a year later, in Darjeeling, India. She learned Bengali, the local language and then taught school. She took her vows for becoming a nun in 1931 and chose Teresa as her name. She became a headmistress at an eastern Calcutta school after teaching for several years. After leaving home and becoming a missionary, she did not see her sister or mother again.

What did she do?

. . . .

When she turned 36, she received the message from God to help India's poor. After receiving fundamental medical training, she then started helping sick and needy people.

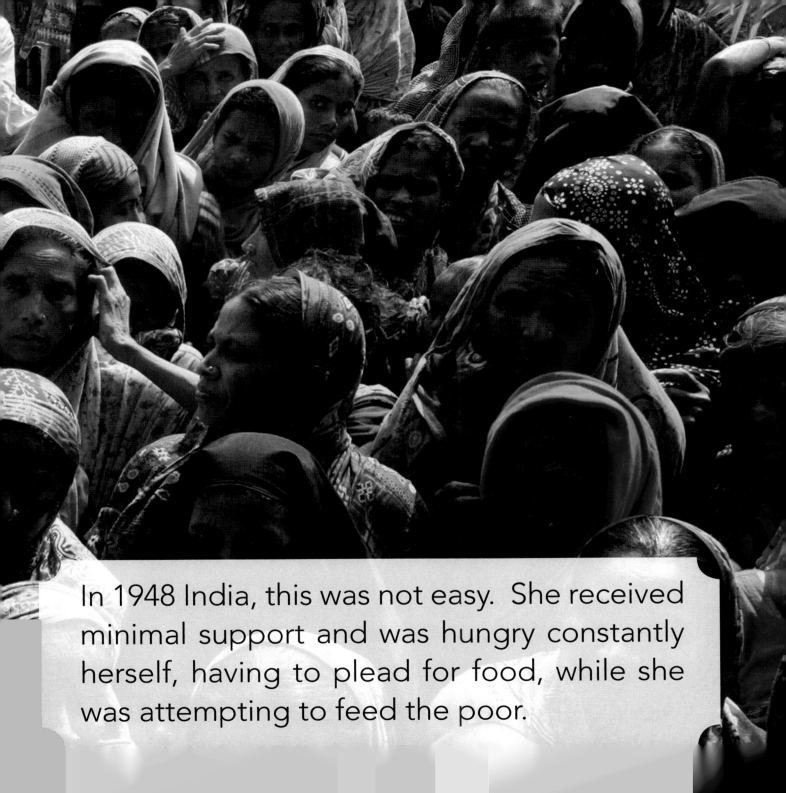

In 1948 India, this was not easy. She received minimal support and was hungry constantly herself, having to plead for food, while she was attempting to feed the poor.

Missionaries of Charity

. . . .

She formed the group called the Missionaries of Charity in the Catholic Church in 1950. She described its purpose as an association taking care of "the hungry, the naked, the homeless, the crippled, the blind, the lepers, all those people who feel unwanted, unloved, uncared for throughout society, people that have become a burden to the society and are shunned by everyone".

Sisters of Charity

She had lofty ambitions, wouldn't you agree? Think about it! Considering that she had been begging for food only a couple of years prior, she had some great accomplishments. There was a mere 13 members when the Missionaries of Charity was started.

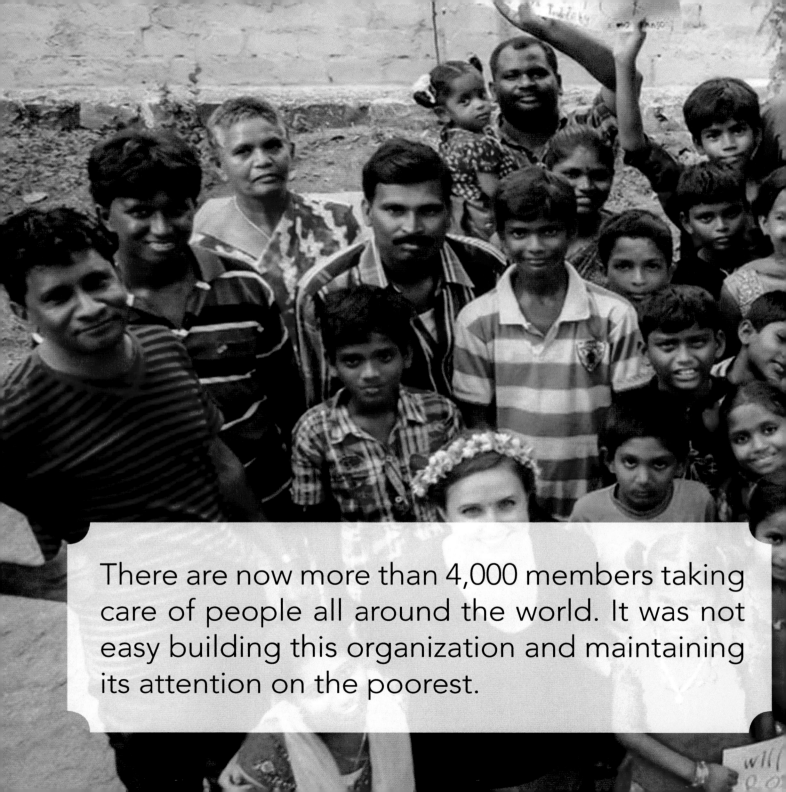

There are now more than 4,000 members taking care of people all around the world. It was not easy building this organization and maintaining its attention on the poorest.

She was able to work almost to the date of her death. It now takes approximately nine years to be a member of the Missionaries of Charity.

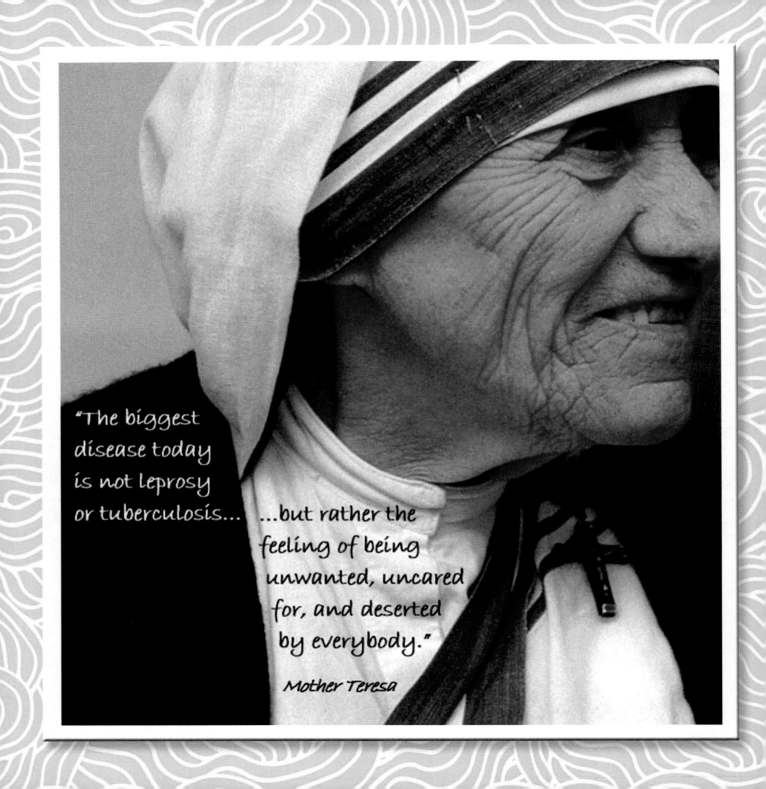

"The biggest disease today is not leprosy or tuberculosis... ...but rather the feeling of being unwanted, uncared for, and deserted by everybody."

Mother Teresa

International Charities

. . . .

One of her quotes was "By blood, I am Albanian. By citizenship, an Indian. By faith, I am a Catholic nun. As to my calling, I belong to the world. As to my heart, I belong entirely to the Heart of Jesus." She could speak Bengali, Hindi, English, Serbian, Albanian, and Bengali which would come in handy on her humanitarian trips outside of India.

At the peak of the Siege of Beirut in 1982, she rescued 37 kids from a front-line hospital by brokering a brief cease-fire between the Palestinian guerrillas and the Israeli army. She was accompanied by the Red Cross, and travelled through this war zone to get to the hospital to remove these young patients.

During the late 1980s, as Eastern Europe experienced more openness, she extended her energies to Communist countries which had previously rejected the Missionaries of Charity. She then started dozens of projects, undeterred by disapproval of her stances against divorce and abortion: "No matter who says what, you should accept it with a smile and do your own work."

Kay Kelly of Liverpool and
Mother Teresa in 1980

U.S Air Force Staff Sgt. Shirly Polk
with 4-year-old Maria

After the earthquake in 1988, she visited Armenia and met Nikolai Ryzhkov, who was Chairman of the Council of Ministers. She also traveled to Ethiopia, assisting the hungry, Chernobyl radiation victims and victims of earthquake in Armenia. She went back to Albania in 1991, where she opened the Missionaries of Charity Brothers in Tirana.

She organized 517 missions by 1996 in more than 100 countries. Her Missionaries of Charity then grew from a mere twelve to thousands, helping the "poorest of the poor" in 450 cities throughout the world.

The first Missionaries of Charity in the United States was founded in New York City's South Bronx area. Nineteen congregations were established by 1984.

Declining Health

· · · · · · · · · · · · · · · · · ·

She experienced a heart attack in 1983 in Rome when she visited Pope John Paul II. After she had another one is 1989, she got an artificial pacemaker. She got pneumonia in 1991 while in Mexico and experienced more heart problems.

Mother Teresa and
Ashwinbhai Mehta

While she offered to tender her resignation, the sisters voted to let her stay, which she agreed to do. During a fall in April of 1996, she broke her collarbone and after four months she got malaria and experienced heart failure. Even with her heart surgery, it became clear her health was declining.

The Archbishop of Calcutta, Henry D'Souza ordered that a priest perform an exorcism when she first became hospitalized with heart problems since he felt that the devil might be attacking her body. He received permission from Sister Teresa prior to performing the exorcism. She resigned from the Missionaries of Charity on March 13, 1997 and then passed away on September 5, 1997.

Father Felix Raj with
Blessed Mother Teresa

At this time, there were over 4,000 sisters and over 300 members of the associated brotherhood, operating in 123 countries with 610 missions. This included homes and hospices for people that had

HIV/AIDS, tuberculosis and leprosy, soup kitchens, schools, orphanages, and programs for family counseling. By the 1990s, they were aided with co-workers numbering over a million.

She lay in repose at St. Thomas, Calcutta, a week prior to her funeral. The Indian government provided a state funeral for her as gratitude for her assistance to the poor. No matter what religion people were, her death was morned throughout the country and in the religious communities. Nawaz Sharif, the Prime Minister of Pakistan considered her "a rare and unique individual who lived long for higher purposes.

Her life-long devotion to the care of the poor, the sick, and the disadvantaged was one of the highest examples of service to our humanity." Javier Perez de Cuellar, a former U.N. Secretary General stated that "She is the United Nations. She is peace in the world."

JU LUTEMI
MOS SHKELNI BARIN

Aeroporti Nen Tereza

Additional Accomplishments

· · · · · · · · · · · ·

In addition to her notable works in helping people, she has also received a few additional accomplishments because of her works. She now has an international airport named for her, Aeroporti Nen Tereza, which is Albania's international airport.

In 1979, when she was received the Nobel Peace Prize, she requested that the dollars involved for the traditional Nobel banquet be contributed to India's poor. In addition to her many awards, she received the Presidential Medal of Freedom from President Reagan.

Criticism of Her Works

· · · · · · · · · · · · · · · ·

In a paper written by Serge Larivée, Geneviève Chénard and Carole Sénéchal, Canadian academics, her clinics received donations in the millions of dollars but lacked systemic diagnosis, medical care, sufficient analgesics, and required nutrition for people experiencing pain: "Mother Teresa believed the sick must suffer like Christ on the cross".

It was thought that any additional money may have been able to transform the poor's health by creating more progressive palliative care facilities. The abortion-rights activists disparaged her beliefs on abortion, and abortion opponents praised her for her fetal rights support.

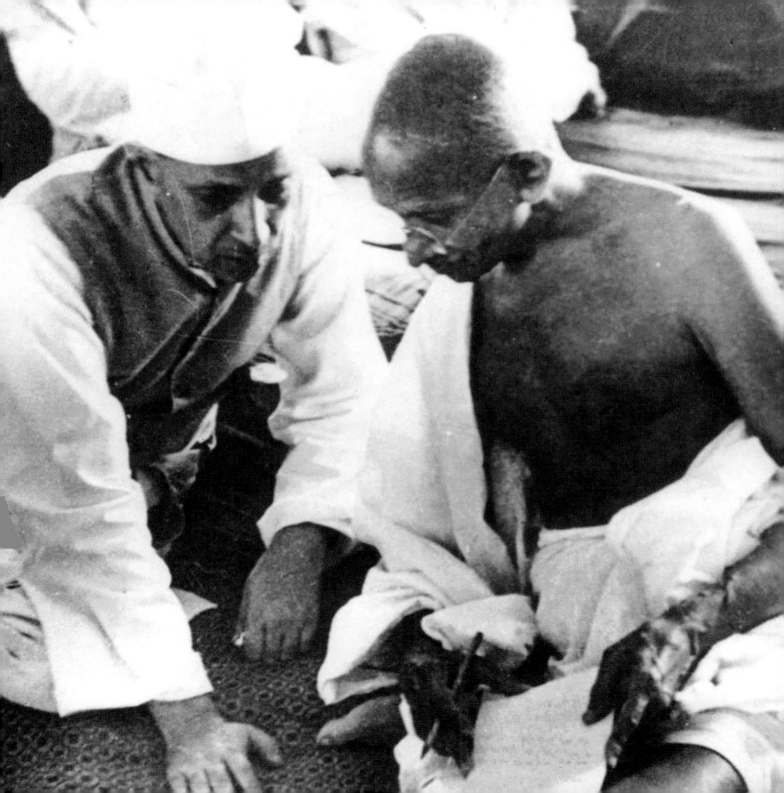

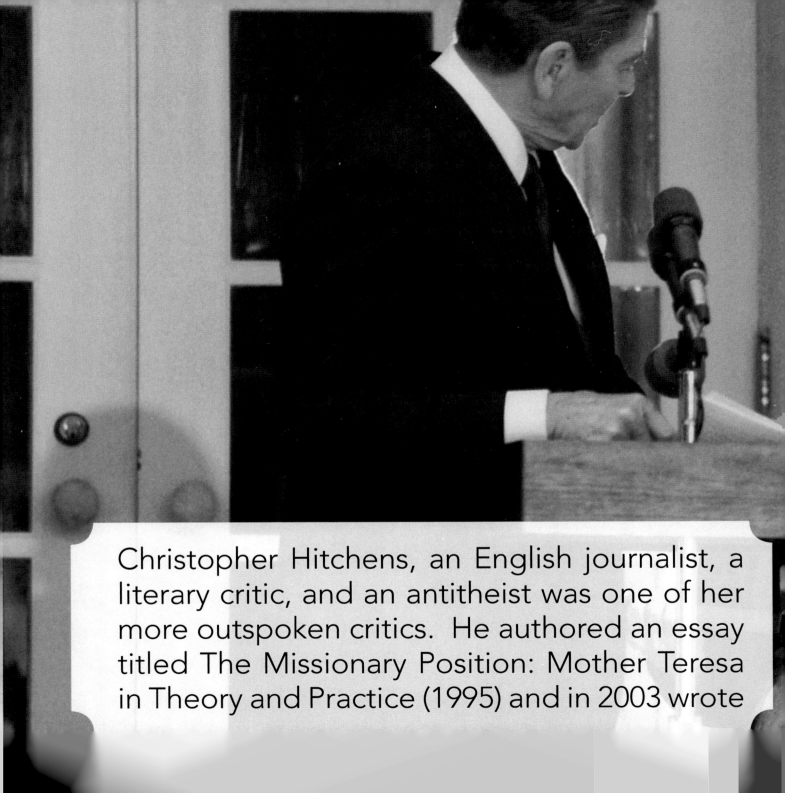

Christopher Hitchens, an English journalist, a literary critic, and an antitheist was one of her more outspoken critics. He authored an essay titled The Missionary Position: Mother Teresa in Theory and Practice (1995) and in 2003 wrote

an article which stated: "This returns us to the medieval corruption of the church, which sold indulgences to the rich while preaching hellfire and continence to the poor.

Mother Teresa was not a friend of the poor. She was a friend of poverty. She said that suffering was a gift from God. She spent her life opposing the only known cure for poverty, which is the empowerment of women and the emancipation of them from a livestock version of compulsory reproduction. He felt that she was a hypocrite for selecting the advanced treatment options for her heart ailment.

While Hitchens felt that he may have been the only one to be summoned by the Vatican, the author of Mother Teresa: The Untold Story, Aroup Chatterjee, was called to provide evidence in opposition to her canonization and beatification; the Vatican abolished its traditional "devil's advocate", serving a comparable purpose.

Hitchens stated "her intention was not to help people", and felt that she was not honest to the contributors regarding how the donations were utilized. He stated "It was by talking to her that I discovered, and she assured me, that she wasn't working to alleviate poverty", and went on to say that, "She was working to expand the number of Catholics. She said, 'I'm not a social worker. I don't do it for this reason. I do it for Christ. I do it for the church.'" His criticism received a comprehensive response by William A. Donohue.

Find more interesting facts about Mother Teresa and her profound works by browsing over the internet and reading related books about her at your local library. You may also ask questions from your teachers, family and friends.

Visit

BABY PROFESSOR
EDUCATION KIDS

www.BabyProfessorBooks.com

to download Free Baby Professor eBooks
and view our catalog of new and exciting
Children's Books